UPSIDE DOWN LIVING

identity & aging

Eleanor Snyder

Herald Press
Harrisonburg, Virginia

Upside-Down Living
Identity and Aging

© 2017 by Herald Press, Harrisonburg, Virginia 22802
    All rights reserved.
International Standard Book Number: 978-1-5138-0170-4
Printed in United States of America

Written by Eleanor Snyder
Cover design by Merrill Miller
Cover photo by Prudencio Alvarez/iStockphoto/Thinkstock

Unless otherwise noted, Scripture text is quoted, with permission, from the *New Revised Standard Version*, © 1989, Division of Christian Education of the National Council of Churches of Christ in the United States of America.

Some Scripture taken from *The Message.* © 2002. Used by permission of NavPress Publishing Group.

For orders or information, call 1-800-245-7894 or visit HeraldPress.com.

20 19 18 17   10 9 8 7 6 5 4 3 2 1

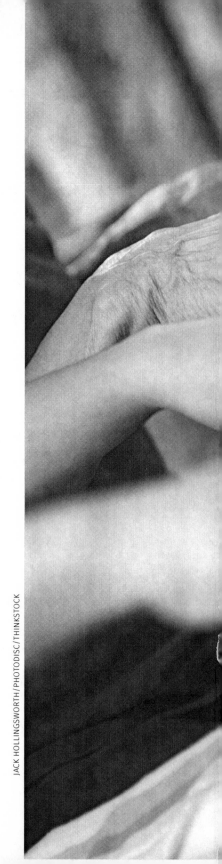

JACK HOLLINGSWORTH/PHOTODISC/THINKSTOCK

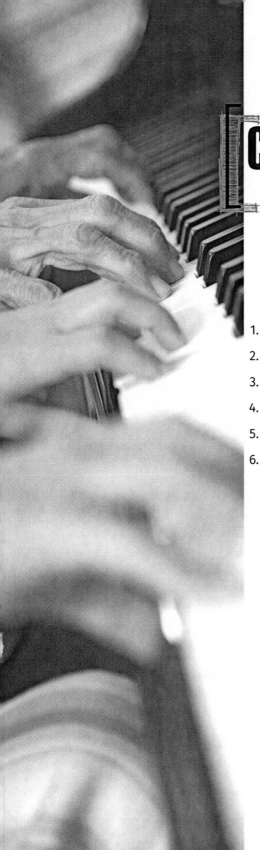

[Contents]

[Introduction]

Becoming Elders

Very few people look forward to getting older, except for children and youth. Yet aging is a fact of life, and according to our greeting card culture, we are over the hill by age forty. The second half of life can be downhill all the way, or it can be an adventure where, when we climb over the hill, we find beauty, grace, joy, and wisdom. We make that choice. When we choose to age gracefully, we do more than survive getting older—we thrive as healthy, mature adults.

Go online or into a bookstore or library and you will find a multitude of resources on healthy aging. They address physical and health issues, as well as the spiritual, psychological, social, and mental aspects of aging.

This study does not attempt to cover these topics in depth. Rather, it provides us with a biblical framework for reflecting on what it takes to thrive in our senior years. Our goal is to become mature adults who can claim the role of elders in our society. Mature adults strive to live with integrity and authenticity. This requires serious soul searching—connecting more deeply with God, letting go of past resentments and hurts, strengthening relationships with family and friends, and reaching out to bring healing and hope in our world.

The Scripture texts may be familiar. Yet they can take on new meaning as we apply them to our older selves. Read them prayerfully. Ponder their meaning. Absorb them as you pray, reflect, journal, dialogue, and engage in spiritual practices. Invite others to study with you, figuring out together how to live as faithful followers of Jesus.

Jesus did not reach old age, but he was wise beyond his years. His teachings show us how to embrace a new way of life in God's alternative reality, the kingdom of heaven. Here is where we gain insights into aging with grace and where we find a supportive group to journey with us through the second half of life. To thrive as elders we need wisdom, grace, and a healthy dose of realistic optimism!

—*Eleanor Snyder*

1

[Surviving and Thriving]

Welcome to a study about how to live the second half of life to the fullest. We are called by many names: baby boomers, midlifers, seniors, zoomers, geezers, retirees, elders, and crones. There is no one-size-fits-all category for this group. In fact, seniors have sometimes been sub-categorized as go-go, slow-go, and no-go—it's not our age but our situation that determines where we fit.

Mature or silent generation		Baby boomer		Generation X		Generation Y		Generation Z	
1930	1940	1950	1960	1970	1980	1990	2000	2010	

Many of you are probably baby boomers, folks born between 1946 and 1964. We are a large cohort that is now in, or moving into, retirement years. We have always been a driving force in society because of our numbers, so it is not surprising that we are redefining aging rather than being defined by it.

> We can choose how we describe ourselves, and so I have chosen the term *elders*. It refers to being older, yet suggests a certain maturity and wisdom.

Traditionally, elders were the old women and men who remembered the past and told its stories, passed on wisdom, and cared for the young and vulnerable. Elders were folks who had done the inner and outer work necessary to grow spiritually, mentally, and emotionally.

> This is our goal—to become wise, mature adults who are true elders in our society.

My siblings and I range both in age and in our approach to aging. We are: a retired teacher who is part of a pastoral team in a congregation, a retired professor who goes to the office every day to do research, a retired nurse who makes and sells crafts when not at her cabin, a retired teacher who travels and tutors English students, a semiretired construction worker, and a farmer. Some of my siblings still work full-time, but I am retired and spend my time reading, volunteering, being with family, and occasionally writing.

How we approach this stage in life, regardless of our situation, is up to us. Moses's invitation in Deuteronomy, for God's people to choose life, holds true for us.

> "I call Heaven and Earth to witness against you today: I place before you Life and Death, Blessing and Curse. Choose life so that you and your children will live. And love God, your God, listening obediently to him, firmly embracing him" (Deuteronomy 30:19-20 *The Message*).

> Are we thriving during this stage of life,
> or are we merely surviving?

Where do you find yourself on each continuum? This study guide is meant to move us toward the right side.

Surviving or thriving chart

Surviving ⟵————————————⟶ Thriving

Fear of change ⟵————————⟶ Anticipation of future

Resistant ⟵———————————⟶ Adaptive

Resentment ⟵——————————⟶ Acceptance

Nostalgia ⟵———————————⟶ Adventure

Anxiety ⟵————————————⟶ Excitement

Stagnant ⟵———————————⟶ Creative

Negative ⟵———————————⟶ Positive

Regret ⟵————————————⟶ Appreciation

Depression ⟵——————————⟶ Joy

Diminishment ⟵—————————⟶ Freedom

Society has its assumptions about aging that are not always life-giving. Christians, however, claim a different outlook on life, an outlook that is based on God's vision for humanity. God calls young people and old people alike to be countercultural, to follow the ways and teachings of Jesus, not the ways and teachings of the world.

Jesus invited his disciples to be part of God's realm, which he called "the kingdom of God" or "the kingdom of heaven." What did he mean? If we respond to this invitation, we opt to submit to God's will in our lives. We follow in the way of compassion, justice, and peace that Jesus modeled. And we believe that God is here among us, nudging us to seek and find abundant life.

"The kingdom of heaven is like treasure hidden in a field, which someone found and hid; then in his joy he goes and sells all that he has and buys that field" (Matthew 13:44).

"For where your treasure is, there your heart will be also" (Matthew 6:21).

"The kingdom of God is among you" (Luke 17:21).

Scripture calls us to accept our lives as a treasure of great value, which God is holding out to us. However, we must act to receive it. We must let go of what prevents us from claiming this treasure. As we age, we no longer seek material possessions. In fact, we are in a downsizing mode. But when it comes to our inner resources, we hope to increase their value. To find this inner treasure, our true elder self, requires serious soul work. We do not come to maturity automatically as we age. During these years we are called to seek the treasures of the heart, precious gifts such as wisdom, insight, grace, and hope. These are the gifts we hold dear and pass on to future generations as our legacy.

We are not alone in God's realm, but part of a community of disciples. We look to this community to find spiritual companions to walk with us in this adventure through the second half of life. Hopefully we find others in our church community who share our values and desire to live the countercultural way of discipleship. If not, we can look further afield to find a small group to help us reflect on aging with grace. Spiritual directors, mentors, and therapists can walk with us as we do this sacred work. If we do not know anyone, we can seek God's guidance in printed resources on spirituality and aging. Journaling is another way to gain insights into our inner life and the nudging of the Holy One in our lives. Regardless of how we do this inner work, may we rest in God's loving embrace as we experience the wonder and joy of aging.

[Talk about It]

▶ Review the "Surviving or thriving chart" (page 9). Mark where you are on each continuum. Are you satisfied with where you are, or would you like to be somewhere else on a continuum?

These suggestions are for individual or small group reflection. Pick and choose what works best for you. If part of a small group, outline rules and expectations for this study, such as confidentiality, honesty, accountability, and integrity.

▶ Sit silently with the Scriptures on page 10. Imagine being the *treasure* that God so joyfully discovers. How does this make you feel?

▶ Gather photos of yourself as a child, youth, and adult. Or, find a set of nesting dolls and allow each doll to represent a stage in your life. Look at each photo or doll and think about your life during that time. What were you doing? What do you cherish about those years? Think about the changes in your life. Think about the core that has always been the real you. Offer a prayer of gratitude for who you are.

▶ Light a taper candle as a symbol of your life, letting the flame represent the divine light within you. Watch the flame, noting how it constantly changes but does not diminish even as the candle grows shorter. Reflect on the candle of your life. What are your hopes for the time you have left?

▶ Affirmation of aging: Place a scarf, shawl, or favorite shirt around your shoulders as a mantle of elderhood. Sit quietly in God's loving embrace. How would you like to honor this stage in your life? What do you need to become a thriving elder? Hear these words: "You are God's beloved treasure. Grow in the light of God's love."

2:

[Letting Go and Embracing]

Have you recently walked into a room and then asked yourself, "Now, why did I come here?" Or have you met acquaintances but were unable to recall their names?

During the second half of life we face countless losses, from small, subtle memory loss to life-altering, punch-in-the-stomach catastrophes. The list of losses we can experience is long and varied—physical, intellectual, financial, relational, emotional, even spiritual. We grieve the death of a spouse, parent, or close friend. We mourn our lost identity and status when we retire or when we lose a spouse.

> Our hopes and dreams are dashed by circumstances beyond our control. How do we cope? From where do we get the strength to move through our losses and see the positive aspects of being an elder?

We have choices in how we deal with losses. With patience, courage, and creativity, we can welcome and embrace the new path that awaits us.

While they were in their early sixties, Fred and Susanne had good, but busy, jobs in the medical profession. They planned to retire within the next year and spend six months traveling around the world before settling into their new normal as retirees. Their dreams were dashed when Susanne was diagnosed with pancreatic cancer and died a few months later. Fred was devastated; his dream future was denied him. Eventually Fred surfaced from his grief. He joined a volunteer group of retired medical professionals who provided medical aid in clinics in Africa. Now he coordinates these trips. He is content with his life and grateful for his health and new community.

Joanne is a single-again woman in her mid-fifties, divorced after thirty years of marriage. Because of her changing financial circumstances, she was forced to move to a small apartment and find a job. She left her church community behind because her former spouse attended there. Some friends abandoned her; others she "dumped." On many levels her future looked grim. But Joanne is a resilient woman. She set about to reinvent herself— she lost weight, joined a gym, found a new church community, and reached out to other single women. She found a group of friends who became her close-knit support group. She is happy in

her new life. She let go of her old life and fully embraced a new,
life-giving identity.

Fred and Joanne suffered profound losses in their second half of
life. But they chose **life over stagnation**, contentment over
despair. They took charge of their own future and now live confi-
dently as thriving elders.

As we age we will continue to face more losses. Grieving them
is natural and healthy. If we become stuck in our grief and disap-
pointment, our lives are diminished. The prophet Isaiah reminds
us that we are not alone in our suffering.

> God created us in love and does not abandon us
> when we face loss.

Do not fear, for I have redeemed you;
I have called you by name, you are mine.
When you pass through the waters, I will be with you;
    and through the rivers, they shall not overwhelm you;
when you walk through fire you shall not be burned,
    and the flame shall not consume you.
For I am . . . the Holy One . . . your Savior. . . .
Because you are precious in my sight,
    and honored, and I love you . . .
Do not fear, for I am with you.
(Isaiah 43:1-5)

Scripture assumes that we will suffer in life. It is not *if* but *when*
tough things happen to us that we can know God is with us. We
need not be overwhelmed nor consumed by our losses when we

remember that the One who created us in love is always present with us. We are very precious in God's eyes.

When we claim our identity as citizens of God's loving reign, we can be assured of God's loving presence through thick and thin. This gives us confidence to accept our aging years with a healthy, positive attitude.

> "The glory of youths is their strength, but the beauty of the aged is their gray hair" (Proverbs 20:29).

Rarely do we find the words **beauty** and **aged** in the same sentence, especially in our society, where beauty, power, and productivity seem to belong to the younger generations. When we look in the mirror, can we see the beauty in our wrinkles, gray and thinning hair, sagging bodies, low energy, arthritic muscles and bones? Yes, we can! For our beauty emanates from within; it is not skin-deep. We are not defined by our physical challenges, but by our attitudes toward them. We can change the script by redefining aging positively and living accordingly.

> "For the kingdom of God is not food and drink but righteousness and peace and joy in the Holy Spirit" (Romans 14:17).

As citizens of God's realm we are part of God's big picture. Right living, peace, and joy are trademarks of life in God's rule. As joy-filled citizens we can extend these traits to our aging selves as well as to others.

> "Gray hair is a crown of glory; it is gained in a righteous life" (Proverbs 16:31).

Letting go of whatever inhibits growth is spiritual work. As we make peace with past regrets and let go of attitudes and beliefs that no longer serve us, we become whole and mature elders. We only have one life to live; let's embrace it fully, regardless of our circumstances.

[Talk about It]

▶ Take an inventory of your recent losses and struggles with aging. On a piece of paper, list personal losses during the last five to ten years. These losses can be about self-identity, relationships, finances, health, work, or other items. Jot down how you felt. On a second piece of paper, list what you have gained during the same time. These gains can be about retirement activities, hobbies, relationships, or other areas. What gifts have you received from these gains? On a third piece of paper, write things you would like to do in the next five to fifteen years. How can you make these possibilities become reality?

These suggestions are for individual or small group reflection. Pick and choose what works best for you.

▶ From your experience, which losses are most difficult for you: physical, emotional, spiritual, or mental? How have you experienced God's presence during times of loss?

▶ Do you know older people who have experienced serious losses, yet remain positive? What is their secret? How can they serve as mentors for graceful aging despite losses?

▶ Conduct a ritual of letting go. Use a stone to represent a loss you need to leave behind: Gently hold the stone in your hand as you think about the loss. Place the stone in a flower bed, in water, in the soil, wherever works best for you. With this act you are choosing to move forward, embracing new life ahead.

▶ Guided imagination. Sit with the Isaiah text on page 15. Imagine God saying these words to you. Insert your name after each *you*. Picture God's visible presence in your struggle with loss. Rest in God's loving promises to you. How do you respond? Option: Take a walk with Jesus. Speak to him of your losses. Invite his counsel on how you can become an elder living fully and faithfully in God's realm.

▶ Affirmation of aging. Wrap yourself in a scarf, shawl, or shirt, your mantle of elderhood. Sit quietly, knowing that you are being wrapped in God's embrace. Hear these words of love: "You are precious in God's sight, and honored, and God loves you. Do not fear, for God is with you."

[3 ̊]
[Investing in
Relationships]

Valuing Our Relationships

"Make new friends but keep the old: one is silver and the other gold." This fun campfire song takes on new meaning as we age. Our friendships become more precious; our relationships become valued, like sacred treasures.

Relationships are important throughout all stages in life. From significant people we learned life lessons about love, loyalty, trust, betrayal, forgiveness, compassion, and respect. As we grow older and sift through our memories, both positive and negative experiences may surface. Another task of this stage is to assess our current relationships. Take an inventory of the contents of your relationship treasure chest.

RELATIONSHIP TREASURE CHEST

Which relationships do you still value?
Which are tarnished and require polishing?
Which are broken and need attention?

As we conduct our relationship inventory, we celebrate the life-giving ones and face regrets for the fractured ones. We take ownership for failing others. We forgive others for failing us. Where possible, and here we must be realistic, we try to mend or renegotiate relationships we want to strengthen.

> Relationships change as we age. These changes affect marriage partnerships, interactions with children, and how we relate with families of origin.

Will is recently retired and happy to leave the work world. But now, with time on his hands and no hobbies, he wonders what to do. He misses his former social interactions. He wants his spouse, Maggie, to do things with him all the time and to plan an active social life for them.

Maggie has her routines for housework, exercise, lunch dates, and volunteering. She resents Will's "interference" in her schedule. She expects him to figure out retirement for himself, just as she did. She feels that their time together can be their usual church and family interactions.

Their frustrations around Will's retirement took them to a marriage therapist, who advised them to renegotiate their partnership. By doing this hard work, they strengthened their marriage relationship and laid the foundation for sustaining a loving partnership in the future. They became more open and honest in expressing their feelings and expectations. They have separate private spaces and are more flexible with their time alone. They enjoy doing more things together.

Maggie and Will met with their adult children to talk about the fact that they now have more time and energy to help where needed. However, they wished to set boundaries for the sake of everyone. As grandparents, they did not want to interfere with their children's parenting; nor did they wish to feel used or merely tolerated by their children. By clearly communicating their feelings and expectations, they laid a foundation for solid adult relationships based on mutual respect and love.

Maggie and Will worked hard to strengthen family relationships. Sometimes, though, it is not possible to fix broken relationships, because of death or resistance by the other party. When that happens, we look elsewhere and choose the "family" we need to sustain and care deeply for us.

Jesus expanded the definition of family. Anyone who
follows God's ways becomes part of a larger family, made up of God's kin, people who love God and care for each other. Friendships of a kingdom nature are different from those we find on social media, where you can be unfriended with a single click.

In God's expansive realm we find mutual love, respect, accountability, compassion, forgiveness, and joy.

> "'Who are my mother and my brothers?' And looking at those who sat around him, he said, 'Here are my mother and my brothers! Whoever does the will of God is my brother and sister and mother'" (Mark 3:33-35).

A wise teacher once stated, "Faithful friends are a sturdy shelter: whoever finds one has found a treasure. Faithful friends are beyond price; no amount can balance their worth" (Sirach 6:14-15).

Older people who are blessed with a network of good relationships will attest to this saying. One close intimate friend is precious; several friends are gifts to be treasured. Jesus was no exception. Though he was God's beloved Son, he depended on close friends to nurture his human self.

> "[Jesus] entered a certain village, where a woman named Martha welcomed him into her home. She had a sister named Mary, who sat at the Lord's feet and listened to what he was saying" (Luke 10:38-39; see also Luke 10:40-42; John 11; and John 12:1-5).

Jesus had a close friendship with Mary, Martha, and Lazarus, three siblings who had a home in Bethany. Jesus was welcomed in their home, where he could relax, eat Martha's good food, and enjoy quiet, meaningful conversations with friends. They loved and trusted each other. They talked about spiritual matters and what they believed. They wept when Lazarus died. Martha was one of the first friends of Jesus to acknowledge his divinity. Mary, in an intimate gesture of love and generosity, emptied a jar of precious perfume on Jesus' feet and then wiped his feet with her hair. More grieving was in store as the siblings saw their friend move toward his death. But during Jesus' life, these three close friends provided him with a safe haven from his itinerant life.

> Investing the time and energy in deepening relationships is crucial for healthy aging.

Our circle of friends may diminish, but it can become more intimate and meaningful. Even one loving, honest friend can make a difference. If we relocate, it takes effort to reach out and transform strangers into friends. It may be a challenge to find a circle of friends who share our dreams, values, and interests, but it is well worth the effort.

[Talk about It]

> These suggestions are for individual or small group reflection. Pick and choose what works best for you.

▶ Think about your friendships. Describe qualities of a faithful friend. How are friends like treasures? Share how you found your friendships. Where would you encourage older adults to find new friends?

▶ Think about your family. Are there ways you can strengthen relationships with your siblings? With your adult children?

▶ Illustrate your network of relationships. On a piece of paper, draw and label circles to show the different groups of which you are a part (work friends, sports team, family, church friends, book club, and other groups). Use crayons or colored pencils to color each circle, choosing colors that reflect your emotional attachment to each. As you color, thank God for the gift of these relationships. You may want to share your circles with someone and explain what the groups mean to you.

▶ It takes maturity and courage to confront someone with past hurts or resentments. How have you approached, or how might you approach, someone who has hurt you, in an effort to try to mend the relationship? What can you do to make amends with family members or people whom you have hurt? Share your experiences and ideas.

▶ Practice forgiveness and release. Hold a long-stemmed rose in your hand. Have a bowl of water on hand. Or, preferably, do this ritual outdoors near water. Whom do you wish to forgive and release? As you think of this friendship, drop a petal in the water for each positive memory. When you are left with only the prickly stem, recall the hurtful aspects of this relationship (grudges, disappointments, hurts). Cut the stem into pieces and drop them in the water. Dispose of the petals and stem in nature with the assurance that it, and you, will be transformed into new life.

▶ Affirmation of aging. Wrap yourself in your mantle of elder-hood. Sit quietly, resting in God's embrace. Hear these words of love: "You are God's treasured friend. God forgives you and heals you."

4

Resting and Soul Tending

Many people these days claim to be spiritual, but not religious. They no longer attend worship services or affiliate with a church. They find little meaning in the traditions of the church, yet insist they have a deep and meaningful relationship with the Divine.

During the second half of life, we grow spiritually as we find our own ways to connect with God and as we participate in a church community. While corporate worship experiences are still meaningful, some older adults feel drawn to a more contemplative spirituality. Still others want to do rituals and prayers outside the Christian religion.

Exploring our inner spirit may be an extension of what we already do, or it may be a whole new adventure. It takes time to sift through the values and beliefs that have served us well in the past. As we age, our values and beliefs are called into question and need to be examined. It is time to remove any obstacles that prevent us from deeply connecting with God.

> By carefully tending our inner spirit, we will be grounded in a belief system that can move into our future with clarity and purpose.

Richard, recently retired, participated in a silent weekend retreat with a desire to deepen his relationship with God. Retreatants were instructed to let go of any personal goals and spend their time listening to, and being with, the Divine. Richard hiked the trails in the autumn woods, sat beside the rippling river, walked the outdoor labyrinth, and practiced mindful eating. In the evenings, he doodled, wrote in his journal, and rested. It seemed as though he was doing nothing, but there was much going on in his inner life. He returned home feeling renewed and more connected to both God and his true self.

About ten years ago, I became part of a small group who audaciously named ourselves wise women. We attended the same congregation and serendipitously found each other. We longed for something deeper than worship and adult education could offer. We meet monthly in each other's homes, catch up on our lives, then spend time doing "soul work." Here is a safe space to ask our faith questions, examine our beliefs, share our personal experiences of the Divine, pray together, and commiserate about aging. We spent a few years reading and discussing *The Gift of Years* by Joan Chittister (Novalis, 2008). We hold each other accountable and maintain confidentiality for what is said.

Over the years we've held rituals for special birthdays, mourned the deaths of parents, celebrated the births of grandchildren, and survived broken relationships and broken bones. We care deeply and look out for each other. I credit the group for encouraging me to draw closer to the source of love. I have been blessed immensely by this spiritual friendship.

> Jesus knew the value of both solitude and community.

Jesus took time from his hectic schedule to spend time alone with God, often out of doors. There, he gained the inner strength needed to continue his mission, doing what God asked of him. Jesus encouraged his followers to do the same.

> "The apostles gathered around Jesus, and told him all that they had done and taught. He said to them, "Come away to a deserted place all by yourselves and rest a while'" (Mark 6:30-31).

> "I am the true vine, and my Father is the vinegrower. He removes every branch in me that bears no fruit. . . . Abide in me as I abide in you. Just as the branch cannot bear fruit by itself, unless it abides in the vine, neither can you unless you abide in me. I am the vine, you are the branches. Those who abide in me and I in them bear much fruit, because apart from me you can do nothing" (John 15:1-2, 4-5).

When the disciples reported to Jesus about their busy activities, he did not tell them to do more good deeds. Instead, he suggested that they retire to a secluded place to do nothing. He knew they needed to rest and be restored in order to carry on his ministry. They too needed time to abide in God.

Jesus used the metaphor of a vine to help his followers understand what abiding, or remaining, in God meant. God is like a vine grower who carefully tends the vine and its branches, which sometimes require pruning in order to produce good fruit. Jesus is the vine, growing strong and sturdy so that he can hold and nurture the branches. The disciples are the branches, who depend on the vine for nourishment so they can grow and produce fine fruit. There is mutual dependence between the vine and the branches. The vine grower oversees the growth, doing what is necessary to produce quality fruit. All three entities thrive because they are interconnected. This is what abiding looks like.

> When we take time to abide in God, we can discover what our souls need to become spiritually mature.

As members of God's vineyard, we may experience pruning in our inner lives. It may mean enlarging our image of God, or redefining our belief system, or using different language to express our spirituality, or experimenting with different spiritual practices.

In God's realm, we are connected to others. We look for spiritual companions to walk with us if such soul tending is new territory. We look for soul mates to practice spiritual disciplines with us and offer safe space for us to explore and deepen our relationship with God.

[Talk about It]

▶ Connect with God in nature. Spend time outside, paying attention to your senses. Share about a place in nature where you feel God's presence, and explain how nature tends your soul.

> Spend time soul tending by doing some of these spiritual practices. They will help guide you to *knowing* God rather than just knowing *about* God.
>
> These suggestions are for individual or small group reflection. Pick and choose what works best for you.

▶ Spiritual reading. What Scriptures draw you closer to God? Some look to the Psalms for daily nurture; others use daily reading guides. There is an abundance of writings on contemplative spirituality, meditation, and spiritual practices. If you have a favorite author, read a selection to the group.

▶ Read Scripture prayerfully. Slowly read one of the suggested verses a few times. What word or phrase stands out? What might it mean for you personally? Rest quietly in God's presence. Share if you wish.

"In returning and rest you shall be saved; in quietness and in trust shall be your strength." (Isaiah 30:15)

"Be still and know that I am God!" (Psalm 46:10)

▶ Meditation and mindfulness exercises help us slow down in body, mind, and spirit and teach us to live in the present moment. We become more aware of what distracts us and what draws us closer to God. When we "do nothing" with God, we are doing much for our spirit. Spend some time being quiet. An option is to do mindful walking. Take a slow walk outdoors, concentrating on your footsteps and breathing. Be aware that God is present all around you and within you.

▶ Affirmation of aging. Wrap yourself in your mantle of elderhood. Sit quietly, resting in God's embrace. Ponder the meaning of this quote for your life now:

"Just to be is a blessing. Just to live is holy." (Abraham Joshua Heschel)

5 Vocation and Volunteering

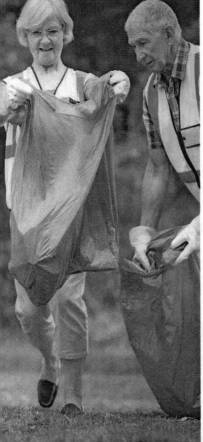

When we enter our retirement years,

we wonder what we will do with all our spare time. We may have unfinished projects to complete, and perhaps more freedom to work on our bucket list. For some of us, time flies just as quickly as it did while we were working. For others, the days stretch out with nothing to do.

Elders who thrive gain much satisfaction from participating in volunteer activities. We do a lot of good-for-nothing (we don't get paid) and are happier and healthier because we volunteer. Volunteers are priceless!

It takes time to get into the rhythm of retirement.

Our society depends on the volunteer services of older people. We provide care for elderly folks and children, help at thrift stores, serve on committees, and deliver meals, books, or other necessities. We have time to give to people in need.

George retired from his job as a house builder because of arthritis. He loved his work, gaining much satisfaction from guiding the projects from start to finish. For him, the future looked bleak. Time stretched out for him; boredom and apathy became his companions. Concerned for his well-being, George's friends persuaded him to spend a week with a relief organization fixing

homes destroyed by flooding. In no time, George was hooked and he joined the organization. Because of his prior work experience, he soon became project manager at building sites. He has a new purpose in his life: providing shelter for those in need. He is happy to use his lifetime skills to serve others.

Marilyn worked as an accountant for a religious nonprofit association. When she retired, she was not surprised when her congregation asked her to volunteer as church bookkeeper/treasurer. Though she liked working with numbers and loved her church, she declined the invitation. She wanted to explore new opportunities for service, preferably in the secular world. Since she loved to cook and bake, Marilyn decided to volunteer at the local soup kitchen. She now enjoys honing her culinary skills and spending time visiting with the meal guests and other volunteers from her community.

The second half of life gives us time and opportunities to work at our relationships with God, family, friends, and our inner being. But our worldview expands beyond deepening relationships. We are ready to look outward to give more of ourselves in service to others. This act of giving back to others is called *generativity*. As mature adults we want to do what we can to leave the world a better place.

> Spending time "abiding in God" can help bring clarity and purpose to how we can engage in the hurting world around us.

["You are the light of the world. A city built on a hill cannot be hid. No one after lighting a lamp puts it under the bushel basket, but on the lampstand, and it gives light to all in the house. In the same way, let your light shine before others, so that they may see your good works and give glory to your Father in heaven" (Matthew 5:14-16).]

This text is part of Jesus' **Sermon on the Mount**, where he taught his followers about kingdom living. Jesus said he was the light of the world (John 9:5), shedding God's love on the people he taught, healed, and confronted. He challenged the disciples to become beacons of light so that all could see the goodness of God. By signing on with Jesus, followers become light-bearers of the good news of God's reign proclaimed by Jesus.

[Transformed by the light, we reflect it in our actions and the way we live.]

It is our acts of kindness and compassion that draw others into God's realm. They are creating a bit of heaven on earth. The kingdom of heaven expands as we do justice, love kindness, and walk humbly with our God (Micah 6:8). The way of discipleship for mature elders is one of balance and integrity, in our inner and outer worlds, in our being and doing. We walk the talk; we practice what we preach.

Only when we know ourselves as God knows us can we fulfill our calling to care for others.

> "The place God calls you to is the place where your deep gladness and the world's deep hunger meet."
> —Frederick Buechner, writer and theologian

Our calling or vocation is what activates us to live out God's desire for us. For some of us, our calling may mean caring for a loved one who needs our time and attention. It may not be what we had anticipated, but it is our reality, and we accept it as a calling. Some of us will happily offer the skills and experiences we have from our work life. Some of us will do creative and surprising deeds that we would not have imagined before retirement. When we do what gives us joy and satisfaction, we are graciously extending God's hospitality.

There are many opportunities to be light for others; remember that even a small match lights a dark area. In reality, our energy, health, finances, life experience, and family situations will dictate how we spend our volunteer time. With the time we have, the task of the thriving elder is to do something that will contribute to making the world a better place. It may mean sitting with a lonely senior or rocking a baby. It may mean using artistic skills, such as quilting or furniture making, to create beauty, from which others benefit. It may mean traveling overseas to live and work with poor people, or protesting injustices at home. It may mean having tea with a lonely neighbor. Mother Teresa once said, "It is not the magnitude of our actions, but the amount of love that is put into them that matters."

[Talk about It]

▶ Make a list of all your volunteer activities. Highlight the ones that give you the most satisfaction, and share why. Are they in line with your passions? How does your faith motivate you to serve others through volunteering?

> These suggestions are for individual or small group reflection. Pick and choose what works best for you.

▶ What opportunities for service might stretch you? Brainstorm out-of-the-box volunteer possibilities that could inspire you and deepen your faith.

▶ Sit with the quote from Frederick Buechner (page 35). What does it mean for you? Then journal, draw, create a collage, or find another hands-on way to help you discern your inner calling. Test the calling with a close friend.

▶ Give yourself a caring hands massage. As you spread lotion or oil on your hands, slowly massage each finger and then your hands. Think of the ways your hands express care for others (sewing, writing, feeding, and other ways). Think of the feelings that are generated by your hands (healing, strength, love). Express gratitude for the gift your hands bring to others.

▶ Reflect on being light. Light a small tealight from a pillar (Christ) candle. Notice how the light diminishes the darkness. Imagine many lights shining in God's realm, glowing brightly, making a difference in the world. How will you use your energy, passion, or gifts to activate the flame of God's light? Carefully blow out the flame. As the smoke dissipates, imagine the Spirit spreading the warmth of your generosity all around.

▶ Affirmation of aging. Wrap yourself in your mantle of elderhood. Sit quietly, resting in God's embrace. Hear Jesus' words adapted from Luke 6:45: "You are a good person, producing good, out of the good treasure of your heart."

6 :
[Living and
Lasting Legacy]

Getting older and wiser are not mutually exclusive. The aging process follows a natural course; however, to gain wisdom requires intentional inner work. Over the course of this study, we have been encouraged and challenged to look inward and reassess our relationships, personal spirituality, and engagement with the world. We have had opportunities to confront our aging and to let go of what stands in the way of becoming thriving elders.

Traditionally, elders had a definite role to play as they served as mentors and spiritual guides to younger generations. Sadly, our current youth-oriented society does not revere its elders in the same way. However, we need not accept ageism; we can reclaim the role of true elders in society. With our knowledge and experience, we have much to offer. The world needs our wisdom.

Roy became a watchdog in the public and political sphere. As a retired journalist, he has some knowledge of what really goes on, so he has become a truth-teller, challenging the rhetoric of the politicians. He encourages older folk to take on a prophetic role in championing social justice issues via letter writing, speaking out, and participating in protest actions. What do we have to lose?

All her life Janet asked questions. She was inquisitive and curious about everything, including her spirituality. She takes time now to reflect on the big questions of life: Why am I here? What is my purpose (God's will)? What is my place in the universe? At her age now, she is comfortable with not knowing the answers. She accepts life as a mystery, filled with divine love, presence, and delightful surprises. Her openness to new possibilities draws others to seek her out for spiritual guidance.

When they retired, Glen and Maggie updated their wills, detailing how to disperse their property and possessions. But they also wanted to leave a spiritual inheritance to their descendants. So they put together a book of memories for their children and grandchildren. Maggie wrote the stories and Glen found the

photos. They included meaningful prayers and songs from the past. They wrote about their spiritual lives and expressed their love to each member of the family.

Kathy feels that her elder calling is to give hope. In finding her calling, she did her inner work of finding her true, authentic self. She spent a long time contemplating, reading, praying, and walking as she pondered her future as a wise elder. She wants to live with integrity and honesty. She wants her words, actions, and attitudes to be in harmony. Her reflections on her past helped her understand and forgive herself. She relies on her intuition and insight to guide her into the future.

Lena is a well-loved grandmother, not only because of her famous chocolate chip cookies. She has given her grandchildren a legacy of unconditional love. There was always time for games, stories, and baking; her being present with them was a precious gift. As they grow older, she stays connected with her grandchildren through social media, sending notes of encouragement and re-minding them of her love and prayers.

Happy are those who find wisdom,
     and those who get understanding,
for her income is better than silver,
     and her revenue better than gold.
She is more precious than jewels,
     and nothing you desire can compare with her.
Long life is in her right hand;
     in her left hand are riches and honor.
Her ways are ways of pleasantness,
     and all her paths are peace.
She is a tree of life to those who lay hold of her;
     those who hold her fast are called happy.
                    (Proverbs 3:13-180

The book of Proverbs is filled with pithy statements about human nature and the ways of God, observed by the sages of old. Wisdom, in this text, is depicted as a woman whose gifts are to be treasured—understanding, long life, intangible riches, honor, joy, and peace.

> This beautiful picture of wisdom becomes visible in God's kingdom.

Jesus, wise beyond his years, used word pictures to describe life in God's realm. His parables, sayings, and stories pointed his followers to a new way of being in the world. In the kingdom, we do not heed the conventional standards, but get a glimpse of how life can be different if ordinary folks like us lived the way God intended. The parable of the sower and the seeds is a prime example of Jesus teaching his disciples about the way of discipleship. This simple nature story had a deeper meaning for his serious followers. Jesus explained it to them:

> " 'To you it has been given to know the secrets of the kingdom of God. . . . The seed is the word of God. . . . But as for that in the good soil, these are the ones who, when they hear the word, hold it fast in an honest and good heart, and bear fruit with patient endurance'" (Luke 8:10-11, 15).

This is a prime example of how Jesus mentored his disciples, sharing his wisdom about God's upside-down kingdom. The disciples needed to "get it" for God's kingdom to grow. They were the receptive soil, the believers who would understand Jesus' message, internalize it, and live it out in their attitudes and actions.

In the kingdom of heaven, love, gratitude, patience, endurance, and honesty are cultivated. We are the seeds who hear God's word and model Jesus' ministry and life. He is our mentor and guide. His legacy lives on in, and through, his followers.

As wise elders, we are charged with telling the stories of God's activity in our lives and planting our seeds of wisdom and insight in our families and in our society. This is our spiritual legacy for those who come after us. Wise elders are living legacies of God's wondrous love.

> "You got me when I was an unformed youth, God, and taught me everything I know. Now I'm telling the world your wonders; I'll keep at it until I'm old and gray" (Psalm 71:17-18 *The Message*).

[Talk about It]

▶ How do you define wisdom? What is the gift of wisdom each elder offers at the beginning of this session (page 39–41)? Who were the wise elders from your childhood, and what spiritual legacy did they give you? What biblical characters are wise elders (e.g., Anna and Simeon)?

> These suggestions are for individual or small group reflection. Pick and choose what works best for you.

▶ Share insights from your experience that have made you wiser. Where do you seek wisdom? With whom, and how, do you impart your wisdom?

▶ Reflect on your spiritual legacy. Do others know you as a spiritual person with deep convictions, beliefs, and values? What do you hope will be said at your funeral? Become a living legacy by sharing what is important to you, now.

▶ Share your insights from participating in this study. What will you take with you? What requires reflection or action?

▶ Affirmation of aging. Wrap yourself in your mantle of elder-hood. Sit quietly, resting in God's love. Hear these words: "Trust in God's wisdom to guide you as you age. God gives you joy, passion, and abundance to live your future with hope."

[About the Writer]

Eleanor Koch Snyder has been retired since 2010. She spent most of her professional career in Christian formation for the Mennonite church in both Canada and the United States, serving in children's ministries and in publishing congregational resources.

Since her retirement, Eleanor spends more time with family and friends both at home and at her rustic cottage on a quiet lake in the middle of the woods. She enjoys traveling, walking, reading, and occasional writing projects.

Eleanor's volunteer activities stem from her love of reading and baking. She is the visiting librarian for a local nursing home, where she selects and distributes books for seniors. She provides "aroma therapy" for a hospice care home, baking goodies for residents and families to enjoy.

Eleanor lives in Kitchener, Ontario, and is a member of Erb Street Mennonite Church.

CPSIA information can be obtained
at www.ICGtesting.com
Printed in the USA
FFOW03n0106210917
40187FF

9 781513 801704